Falling Off by Kathleen Norris

Volume Four in the
Big Table Series of Younger Poets

◘ BIG TABLE PUBLISHING COMPANY/CHICAGO

The Big Table Series of Younger Poets consists of books which have won the annual competition for the most distinguished volume by a younger poet. The competition is open to any poet 35 years of age or under, who has never published a book of poems. Manuscripts must be submitted between August 1 and October 1 of each year; the winning volume appears in the spring of the following year.

Volume One   *The Naomi Poems, Book One: Corpse and Beans*
                  by Saint Geraud (1940-1966)

Volume Two   *We Weep For Our Strangeness*
                  by Dennis Schmitz

Volume Three   *License To Carry A Gun*
                  by Andrei Codrescu

Volume Four   *Falling Off*
                  by Kathleen Norris

Some of these poems appeared in the following periodicals and anthologies and the author wants to thank the editors for their permission to reprint them: *Lillabulero, Tennessee Poetry Journal, The World, First Issue, Sun, Sumac, The Dragonfly* and *Another World.*

Manufactured in the United States of America.

Library of Congress Catalog Card Number: 76-172021

First Printing

ISBN: 0-695-80257-7 cloth
       0-695-80256-9 paper

4

FOREWORD

A cartoon of an angel as a Lolita down on her luck—salacious, self-indulgent and mocking, to be sure, but a bit too plump and vacuous—which Kathleen Norris drew in a letter she sent in February 1971, helped me to realize how vigorously this book resists admiration based too exclusively on the more radiant and mysterious aspects of the angelism in some of the best poems in it. Radiance and mystery, along with a certain elusive tenderness, impressed me immediately when I first read this book in manuscript a few months before the cartoon arrived. But the cartoon sent me back to the manuscript, and the contrary, acerbic and contagious side of her poetry became more evident and valuable. The cartoon shows a teenage angel floating about, sporting wings, halo, curls and a lopsided, faintly derisive grin, wearing an altar-boy shift sufficiently transparent so that breasts and pubic triangle are visible.

Needless to say, the drawing amused the hell out of me. But I also felt a bit let down, even betrayed: the cartoon seemed a bit too cute, smart-ass, smug in its derision and ability to shock. It hardly seemed the work one would expect from a young poet whom one had come to appreciate for poems which talk about the angels as creatures incandescent with secrets, humor and love. This incandescence had so impressed me, in fact, that at one point I suggested to Miss Norris that she consider making a book out of only one poem, the long "Excerpts from the Angel Handbook," or exclusively out of poems about angels, and illustrate it with hundreds and hundreds of pictures of angels from all over the world and from as many civilizations and centuries as possible, including such angels as the Assyrian angel with the long, curled, luxurious beard and the body of a giant bull with wings; and the Angel of Death who appears in processions on certain feast days in Mexico wearing a skull with a cigar clamped between broadly grinning jaws; and Magritte's angel in the business suit and shoes in the gouache "Le Mal du Pays." Such a book might do justice, I felt, to the kind of

radiant, mysterious angelism one finds in lines addressed to an
angel who will visit the earth such as:

> It will often be expedient to remove your wings altogether
> from your back where people will first think to look for
> them,
> and carry them around inside you—
> at such times be careful that your hands do not forget
> and begin to imitate their beating in your heart,
> for if you begin to fly, the police will be called
> and you will only confuse them

and:

> Their logic will not make much sense to you,
> their mathematics especially will seem impossible,
> for you will never be able to divide anything

and especially:

> and your flights (even though you are careful
> to keep them invisible), will sometimes make them sad
> they will not understand that you never go anyplace you're
> not meant to be

It would have been a lovely book. But it might have done more
damage than good, I came to realize, by presenting Miss Norris
in too romantic, if not too tranquil and lucid, a light: the young
poet as acutely sensitive, loving angel, beyond the good and evil
with which we humans must struggle—the young poet as Puck,
shaking her head and murmuring, sadly, without bitterness,
"What fools these mortals be!" What such a presentation would
miss, in effect, are those qualities which the teenybopper angel
with breasts and pubic hair encourages one to pay more atten-
tion to in her work: the quiet sarcasm, if not iconoclasm, the
slow burn, as it were, between the lines, the itchiness, the

bruises, the occasionally waspish, sudden bite. The cartoon is, of course, the witty, abrasive gesture of a young poet who resists being type-cast in any way. And it was as if it were saying about this book: "Sure, some of the lines and stanzas in here are about the radiance and mystery of angelism: but it's also like this, baby." (Ten monsignors faint on the spot.)

Cocteau once preened by confiding: "I have an angel in me whom I am continually shocking." In these poems Miss Norris appears to say the opposite: "The angel in me continually shocks me." And one of the ways this seems to happen is when her angel refuses to conform to stereotype. Instead, the angel may hide its bejeweled wings under her bed, where they gather dust; or its visitation will leave sores on the inside of her mouth; or the angel will receive a lot of business calls.

This kind of surprise is also evident in another quality in her work which I admire a lot and which can be found in some of the angel poems and some of the others as well: and that is, the insistence by the poet to include the most comprehensive dimensions of the experience being explored in her poem. As a result, Miss Norris is able to achieve a peculiar tension, beauty and strength by allowing disparate elements to exist within the same poem or within the same book. One finds, for example, such a wry, scatalogical stanza as the following in "Excerpts from the Angel Handbook":

You may find employment with the Sanitation Department
or at any laundry

and near it such a warm, gentle one as:

At times it will seem that we have deserted you but
when people take you in, you will leave their teacups
        glowing,
their windows shining

7

The same poet can write lines such as, "Something pulls at me so/Gently tending me so/Carefully and/like nothing else/ I move simply/Toward the light" and also "I grow from this darkness/Brutal as a flower"; or "I keep my life secret as I can,/And watch for hours as clouds settle on the city/The way the earth rolls slowly over the dead" and also "You could fuck almost anything." And she is able to create a poem written out of such an exquisite sense of proportion and possible exacerbation of the most sensitive of nerve-ends as "Days like Today" and also such an equally fine poem which comes from a jarring and often ribald sense of disproportion and consistent bad manners toward gentility and life in general as "Her Application to Elysium."

One of the good results from this kind of comprehensive sensibility is that we are able to read poems which convey a beautiful, piercing sense of how alien yet familiar, how lovely, graceful and mysterious, and yet grotesque, awkward and banal must be the worlds in which Miss Norris finds herself—the world around her, as well as the other, more celestial one inside. "That spirit should be united to matter is incomprehensible," Pascal reminds us, "and yet that is the way it is." I suspect that Kathleen Norris feels right at home with the wonder in this aphorism, and she'd also approve, I bet, of Pascal's good sense which encouraged him to keep a sturdy chair nearby at all times so that there'd be something there to block his falling into the Void.

PAUL CARROLL

CONTENTS

"went to sleep in Shreveport, woke up in Abilene"
Bob Dylan

"My life was never so precious
To me as now.
I will have to beg coins
After dark"
James Wright

"let profit be
the love we part with, and failure
the first day of the rest of our lives"
James Tate

for the seaweed harvester

I.

an angel flying slowly, curiously singes its wings
and you diminish for a moment out of respect
for beauty then flare up after all that's the angel
that wrestled with Jacob and loves conflict
as an athlete loves the tape, and we're off into
an immortal contest of actuality and pride
which is love assuming the consciousness of itself . . .

Frank O'Hara
"In Favor Of One's Time"

CELEBRATIONS

THE WINDOW BOX

There is dampness
At my feet   I suspect
That something grows
There and it will soon
Smother me   I wish
I could bend down   just
Begin
To feel the sides
The shapes
Of the sides
And shadow
I wish I could see the other things
In the room and know
What I was;
Something pulls at me so
Gently   tending me so
Carefully and
Like nothing else
I move simply,
Toward the light

THROB

You cut me
Into pieces and
Put them in separate corners
Of the room
Each part
Placed under pillows or
Into water

I grow from this darkness
Brutal as a flower   like
Starfish my fingers know the shape to take again

THE ANGEL

"L'ange avait replie ses ailes pour ressembler à tout le monde"
"L'Ange", Louis Emié

When I died the first time
They made it so I could live cutting under
My skin   putting tubes into my arms
And sides   my body fed
All day   my mouth had one infant syllable
For pain
    My bones never had much of a place to go,
    But I got up this morning   blue crickets
    In my eyes   I look back
    At them and
    In the mirror too
    They shine

The angel
I suspect it has hidden its wings
Under the bed   its bejeweled wings
Gather dust
Under the bed,
My bones forget what they were, fox,
Fish, or tree:
    All night I hung
    By my wrists
    In your room,
    Waiting for this morning

    Eating is so arbitrary

    You fed me soup
    And bread

STOMACH

My stomach is of many minds;
It believes everything it eats.
My eschatological
Stomach, a fundamentalist
Of sorts, grows intent
At drawing blood from
Surfaces of things:
Ice-cold fingers touch its inner lining,
It lives in fear of confusion.

The stomach clenched
Its teeth, its nose bled all day
As I stumbled through snow,
Cracking theories of poetry
Over its skull.
Gilded toothpicks,
Sweet-sour pork
Did a desperate violence
To its body.
It had to be saved, put to sleep,
But it woke early,
Still restless with envy of the resplendent
Spleen.

I will be good to my stomach,
Tomorrow; listen, and believe it
For a while. The stomach
Is serious and unhappy.
It wants to do something really
Symbolic; it wants to be
The ultimate
Stomach.

DAYS LIKE TODAY

On days like today
You have to be especially careful
With your life
This means you can be punished
For preserving it in too extravagant a fashion,
This means that while I'm walking here
Under this perfect circle of trees
Under this perfect circle of sky
There are no clouds,
The sky is outrageously blue, and that even
The shadows are clear:
Nothing to be imagined
Under all this sunlight
If only it would rain or snow,
Anything short of hailstones would comfort me

On days like today
You'll settle for any sign that happens
To come your way:
The stone I had to roll from my stomach
To get up out of bed this morning,
The splinters on the floor
Where it fell, and now this waterfall
Which appears to be a flight of birds

I will put them with the secrets I keep,
Plans to be made;
I can improvise from here

Somewhere there's a life
Of limited possibilities, running down
With all the precision of a well-made watch.
It is full of circumstances, like owning a rug,
That come to mean something over a period of time
And in conjunction with other circumstances,
Such as the existence of bedouins, trees in the forest,
Or apartment buildings.
The world is full of people who haven't died yet,
Who station themselves like Indian tribes
On hills overlooking even the smallest happiness;
They wait for your eventual appearance on the horizon,
Dependent on the weather, the distance traveled, *etc.,*
But it's possible to fool them, to stretch out
For three thousand miles
In any direction,
Leaving an innocent shoe behind in New York City
While dropping a red hat over Kansas.
It is possible to make even the most tender emotions
    impervious
To their bullets, arrows, and spears
By putting on an armor that is lighter than air
Or any other substance,
By being so purely and invisibly present
That they will not think to look for you
As you walk alongside them, or appear in front of them
As a window, or door.
It is possible to move slowly along their bedroom walls
    at night
As they strap themselves down to sleep,
Afraid that the winds could pass through them like death

And they would never know it;
They may wake suddenly, and search for you in the room;
They will find you harboring the most secret and
      perpetual joy
The way a cat keeps an immense space within its eyes,
And turns quickly to reveal it,
And turns away

RUNNING THROUGH SLEEP

I would prefer to live quietly in silks,
Like a lady, in a place where a lady lives,
But I have seen this body I carry around alone;
Streamlined for sleep, its arms, ears, and lips removed,
It resembles a fish swimming through dark water,
Or a fire burning undetected,
Watching everything around it
Turn to soft, wet ash;
It runs faster as the light approaches
Along the edges of its skin,
It tries to recall the shape of a foot,
Or a face smiling in a photograph,
Something it can fit into
So it won't disappear

Sometimes it's no more than a dampness
On the undersides of logs and rocks,
Running without a trace into the earth,
And the roots of plants;
But at night the shoes of people with the sweetest
    laughter,
The gentlest step,
Are shoes with knives in the soles
That can cut three feet deep,
And the heart seeks refuge
In the oldest, smoothest stones

Sometimes it feels like the water forming in clouds,
Commanding a view of whole sides of continents,
And the ocean's edge;
But it fears falling from such a height

And having no place to go;
It fears that the police will find it rummaging
Through someone else's closet,
Stuffing its heart with rags

THE VIEW

Here, where I am,
The light is good
But the windows across the way,
Which ought to reflect it,
Are pale as the eyes of blind men;
And when the wind comes up,
It comes as if nothing were in its way,
As pure as it comes into North Dakota
From across Saskatchewan, and the Canadian tundra,
Where everything is as empty as it should be.
It slips in through the bedroom wall,
And in between the sheets,
Leaving nothing much behind,
Nothing but lampshades, or the hems of curtains,
To hold on to

Some people are born with feelings
Of such great emptiness
That they eat a lot,
Hoping it will make them more significant;
Others have only one eye,
And not much is apparent to them.
There are people whose amazement begins to burden them,
Whose hearts are like the mouths of fish pried open with
    sticks,
And it is easy to see what they see:
You can sit in the middle of the floor,
And wait for the night to end;
You watch the table, the rug, and the chair,
But nothing happens.

You can see that the earth supports the weight of all
    the things on it,
But you notice it is trembling;
You notice in the middle of everything
There are roads that have been unused for centuries,
Spaces a person could step through,
And fall forever

                                              James Wright

Here, no one has diplomatic immunity;
It sometimes takes thirty minutes to go one mile
Traveling at a speed of thirty miles an hour

It rains where it pleases and everything seems spilt
     on the earth,
While the sky creeps slowly
Along the illusion of a horizon, mountain, river,
     field, and fence

Everyone is required to carry at least one postcard picture
     of the scenery in their pockets
Everyone puts on lovers like the overcoats traditional
     in bad storms
Everyone knows that surgery will be necessary someday,
     as sleep is now

I keep my life as secret as I can,
And watch for hours as clouds settle on the city
The way the earth rolls slowly over the dead

WITH YOU

I will sneak by now
While the past is busy completing itself,
Collapsing wherever it can, and accumulating like dust;
It won't see me,
And the future has to support everything that exists,
With its base rising out of the Hudson near
        the Port Authority Bus Terminal,
Its apex hooked on the most distant star;
It can't possibly move.
The trick is to be looking straight ahead
And still keep a solid footing on the surface of the river;
It's easier if I don't carry anything,
Or when you are laughing over on the other side

I make it to the place where I have seen you standing,
And you've already moved on;
I recall a small, tropical paradise
A little to the left;
I find your footprints,
But as I begin to follow them,
They disappear.
I'm on the streets now, just a few minutes from Hawaii,
And it's snowing

When I wake up, there is nothing for miles
But a few half-buried flags raised by the wind
That drift toward the horizon
I have just enough time to fill my pockets with water,
And breathe in

When I wake up there is a seashell in my hand

It was waiting in the desert
Where the tides left it centuries ago,
And now the wind passes through,
Making a sound as if all the ocean were enclosed
    in its emptiness

BEAN SONG

A bean does not know much,
But it remembers the winter.
It sweats in secret, its skin grows tough
And smooth as it pushes up against the darkness,
Against the weight of the universe.
Somehow it displaces just a little earth,
And everything shifts to one side.

The bean flower stands up to see if it is in
        the middle of a field,
Or someone's flower pot;
It is beautiful and bitter,
And dies after a while,
But the bean keeps singing to itself
A song about the stars,
And the cities, and the people
Who live in sunlight;
No one hears it singing,
Only a few ever learn the song:

At night, when I sleep alone,
I sing it for you

EXCERPTS FROM THE ANGEL HANDBOOK

1

Be careful how you unfold your wings—
there are some in the world who are not content
unless their teeth are full of feathers

2

You may find employment with the Sanitation Department
or at any laundry

3

When you ride subways wear ornate silver shoes
and always stand near the door

4

When you cross at intersections look both ways, then up

5

It will often be expedient to remove your wings altogether
from your back where people will first think to
       look for them,
and carry them around inside you—
at such times be careful that your hands do not forget
and begin to imitate their beating in your heart,
for if you begin to fly, the police will be called
and you will only confuse them

6

You will find that you are most free
when you are able to sit still

7

You will have a great fondness for music,
but be sure to hide your ears when listening to it,
for they will throb and grow

8

You must listen to what people say
even when they talk to you: this will involve
keeping silent much of the time, and being bored a lot

9

You will never tell a lie,
but you will have many secrets

10

At times it will seem that we have deserted you but
when people take you in, you will leave their
        teacups glowing,
their windows shining

11

You are not especially alert to danger but at times
you will sense an uncontrollable desire to warn others
of impending doom: to yell "Watch Out!"
as they walk under low hanging branches, or along
     the edges of pits

12

You will meet some who wear their faces nervously,
who will tell you how it seems
they will not survive;
these are the children, they still have parents,
or still need them

13

Many things that you do will seem strange to them:
remember their savage origins,
be gentle and kind

14

Since you find no situation intolerable,
they will think that you are cruel

15

Their logic will make much sense to you,
their mathematics especially will seem impossible,
for you will never be able to divide anything

16

For amusement sometime, look at the picture books:
angels there have huge silver wings, silken robes
and long fine hair, and always look like eunuchs

17

You will meet some whose faces give a glow
as if they once had halos:
these are the lovers,
you will make a lot of love

18

Making decisions will be the most natural of tasks,
but it will rarely seem necessary to make promises,
and it may be difficult for even the lovers to
    live with you;
they will not understand when you get angry
and your flights (even though you are careful
to keep them invisible), will sometimes make them sad
they will not understand that you never go
    anyplace you're not meant to be

II.

"sooner or later, one of us must know"
Bob Dylan

TOMORROW

Tomorrow I said I would fly
Six thousand miles and back
Without eating but it's no use,
Only angels travel light as that
And again this morning
I found myself waking,
Buried under thousands of shoes
On the closet floor;
There will be more of them
Tomorrow; I will need the bags I packed
Years ago, kept locked in the next room
All this time

Tomorrow I said
You could see all the skin
I never showed
On the city streets,
But I think I can tell what will happen;
The explorer arrives by ambulance
Instead of airplane,
And the bandages he brings along
Are heavy, transparent, and useless
As memories

I wish I was like the sky is today,
So sure of itself;
It has no fear like this,
Moving with suitcases
From place to place

TERRIBLE WEATHER

When summer came, everyone said it was the best thing
    that could have happened to winter;
It hung around, warming everything,
But after a while
Even the air lost its independence,
And began to cling to the smallest spaces between elastic
    and flesh;
The birds, sensing imminent disaster,
Refused to fly, and just stepping on the streets
Was extremely dangerous,
All the time you would see people slipping
And sinking helplessly through the pavement

Our mouths grew so full of teeth as we slept
That we choked to death every night;
In the heat it was impossible to tell
If we had become suddenly obese,
Or had grown tiny spines on our arms and legs.
We kept track of everything we used up and later replaced,
We found that it was just as far to the hospital
    around the corner
As to the balcony of the movie theater in the middle of
    the next block

Friends returned to the city
But we did not understand much of what they said to us;
They had grown so large in our minds
That they seemed disgustingly small
Once we saw them again;
We never made love anymore, we moved from room to room
Crowded out by chairs, silverware, and old books;

When a cool breeze came along, we bolted the doors
And sat by the windows, watching;
It began to rain, and I saw you leaving at last,
Setting sail out the window
In a cardboard box
And the water kept on rising, the day got worse and left

THE ARRIVAL OF APRIL

Some kid lets a kite loose
To see what will happen
And he watches it move reluctantly
        past the trees, wavering upwards,
And the afternoon blows past like any other,
I cannot quite determine the direction of the wind

It must be the purest thing;
The sidewalk still cold
And I can hardly walk

I am so light
Nothing holds me here,
And emptiness claims every place I've been

It must be the purest feeling,
April again, beginning to rain

THE BEGINNING OF MAY

I'm not sure if this is the Paris Hotel
Or just a minor form of oblivion

It's like sleeping near the ocean,
Dark water on either side, yesterday, tomorrow

The colors are not ones I would have chosen
But the view overlooking 97th Street and West End Avenue
Is the one I always wanted

It's like taking death in small doses,
Summer is certain as anything

FALLING OFF

I thought it would happen someday
Easily, certainly,
With the aid of a miraculous cancer
Or a needlessly spiteful lover

I expected some signal
So clear and unmistakable
I would recognize it in my sleep
I thought the horizon was a place
That came upon you sooner than you knew,
Where the edge was,
And you had to watch your step

There is nothing now in sight
Except the city, vertical
And bottomless,
Where the worst things happen
And everything stays the same.
What year was it you said,
"You'll need a lot of tedium to get by";
This present moment seems to be lasting forever

"let profit be the love we part with,
and failure the first day of the rest of our lives"
James Tate

It is always the same,
You turn around, and another piece is missing
Yesterday I could see into the corner
For the first time in a year,
Your face as familiar and impersonal as the moon
This morning even the voice was gone,
The room was full of junk

It should be easy,
A look around the room, you get up
And walk around;
You can't tell if it's the airport
Or the hospital,
There are children here
Who never learned to swallow

It doesn't take long to lose track,
You could wake up anywhere,
You could fuck almost anything.
It should be easy, you sort through your emotions,
You get up and feel things,
But you never know exactly
How to break even, moving
From the edge of one edge
To the edge of another

MEMORANDUM

The accountant's notebook

The illusions: they fit like an iron lung, and
can keep you going indefinitely. The persons
suspected of stealing them are to be considered
armed, and dangerous

Little Joe, who was last seen electrocuting himself
by trying to make ends meet

The art of making foods so subtle that even politicians
don't know how to eat them

A little faith: the swimmers here don't seem to know
where the next breath is coming from

FRAGMENT FROM A DEATH FESTIVAL

You have to watch your laughter around here,
It's likely to spill all over everything
And ruin someone's silk and suede burnoose

Here they come, looking like refugees from a mercy killing
There must be childhoods they are trying to forget,
       television, bad food, and fantasies,
Neighborhoods that were not good enough, that they
       never visit now

One changed her name so she could feel like somebody;
By now her face has begun to disappear and the others say,
"the poor oblivious darling, she looks more like a vacuum
       cleaner than a person and I hear there are teeth in her cunt"

They sit around and discuss their histories, which they've
       filled with enough mythology to sustain them
They like the tiny replicas of themselves that shine in each
       other's eyes

HER APPLICATION TO ELYSIUM

It consisted of 8 to 10 pages of short essays,
Much like the applications to colleges such as Bennington,
    or Sarah Lawrence
She wrote that she had always kept a certain distance from
    her surroundings;
This was in response to the first question, requesting name,
    address, and schools previously attended

The enclosed booklist revealed that she had read too many
    French pornographic novels,
And she confessed that she generally did what she was told.
    (This was confirmed by an ex-science teacher who wrote:
      "all she requires is a good slap across the backside,
        and she will move slowly in the desired direction")

When asked about her most meaningful relationships,
She prepared a list, carefully catalogued,
With cross-references:
The female peer, the male peer, the female teacher,
The male teacher, foreign nationals, vibrators of various
    shapes and sizes,
A policeman's horse she had befriended in Central Park,
A museum curator, her local Democratic assemblyman.
She was careful to explain what each symbolized,
    in the long run,
What each experience had done for her

To finish up,
She mentioned several virtues which she felt would
    particularly recommend her to the desired kingdom;
A basic discomfort with things as they are,

The ability to live vicariously,
A limitless capacity for self-pity

She had a friend mail it for her;
And months later, she eagerly opened the little kit,
    which contained some embalming fluid, and a copy of the
    memoirs of Anais Nin,
And her eyes would not stop shining

LUNCH

The game was being played on the surface. One poor girl
had injected herself with embalming fluid only minutes
before, and the effects were just beginning to be felt by
those around her. There were observers too, eyes moving
like birds around the table, mouths busy at their food.
The students were huddled, quite serious. There were lessons
here, to be had for the asking.
The game was lent an aura of silliness by a grown man wearing
a transparent shirt. The game was being played on the surface,
so as to reveal almost nothing, and
deceit had made fools of everyone, except perhaps for
the most deceived, who were never really fooled. The game
was being played on the surface, as if only abstractions
were real. Some feelings were drawn out, startled
to find themselves exposed to the light; they wandered across
the vast expanse of tabletop until they became bored and
eventually quite anxious, and had to be led out, complaining
of a terrible thirst.

THE LOVERS

They measured things so carefully, the time they would
allow for being with each other, and eventually, even for
thinking of one another. There were small, inexpensive
presents they would exchange several times a day, with
little insults, and then larger, more expensive gifts,
which, as they walked through the streets of the city,
would bump sharply down on the pavement, or swipe at the
heads of passers-by. They had learned to live with
boredom, and filled their place with abstract people,
animals, and plants, which to everyone
else looked like pieces of old shirt cardboard. They
"believed in things." They "made eyes." They were aware
of all the obvious holes.

EVAPORATION POEMS

1.

I would like to be as mobile as my mind
I had a religious aunt who was
And of course, she died
(She flew out a window into the Ideal)

So much noise, the water in stems,
The workings of animal teeth
And intestines;
Such foolishness, she decided,
You have to disconnect the pain
From the sense of loss,
Until all you feel is nostalgia and boredom,
Until you're free from distraction

The trouble begins when no one wants anything in particular,
And you have to decide what to give them in return;
"It's like deciding anything," she said,
"Even transformation has its price"

2.

The dead complain of having inadequate information
They've been playing with matches and razor blades for
          some time now, and nothing has been revealed.
They're too aesthetic to pay much attention to detail;
Somehow, though, they've managed to obtain college degrees
And roses spring up in their hair
At the mention of death, or dying

They sense that something perpetual, banal,
And quite routine is going on in the universe
They say it will make them crazy if they don't watch out

They're on the lookout for the future, and its "complications"
If you say that even the water's need is a simple one, they
    get upset

3.

All summer I have watched the water
Take whatever shape it can,
Whispering, "there is the past,
And the future, and between the two of them
You must be careful not to disappear"

Now I see so clearly on the days when rain turns to snow;
The wind passes along the surfaces of things,
The chill settles in around the place where I have moved
    with everything

SOONER OR LATER

We find out in our sleep that nothing ever happens twice

You grow out of your purple suit and I give away all my
     Rolling Stones records
I think, "what's happening here?" You say, "what did
     you expect?"

I don't know whether to sleep like crazy or get up and
     run through the dance routines
You appear in a dream to say, "I can feed you in my shower,
     come on over" and then, "I don't even have a shower,
     I just said that"

III.

MESSAGES

This morning it was the cat with a note that read:
"You have become my latest abstraction"

Yesterday the mailman brought three letters from your lawyer
declaring you to be the sole guardian of my absence

I'm so glad to hear it, I've been wondering what it was you
meant to say: excuse me there's a plane about to crash, writing
something in blue in the air just above my head, there's a woman
who seems preoccupied with being ready at every turn, looking
out of the corner of her eye to see if it's really now
that the blow is about to fall, but it's not me.
For months now, there's been this strange sensation,
someone nosing around the platform after the train has left,
picking up my smell, a few strands of hair, putting them
together, as if they could spell something

I know how carefully you think things out, the way logic
works a little at a time, the subtlest of betrayals,
a terrible form of nostalgia.
I don't know what to say, all the shells on the beach,
apartments kept vacant by greedy landlords, even bodies
left uninhabited, from time to time

I'm listening now to early Dylan, back when people said he
couldn't sing

PLAYBOY: *Let's turn the question around: why have you stopped composing and singing protest songs?*

DYLAN: *I've stopped composing and singing anything that has either a reason to be written or a motive to be sung . . . the word "message" strikes me as having a hernia-like sound . . .*

THE PRODIGY

Indulgence let him get this fat,
His sixteen mothers provided the rest.
That was 1966, things are tougher now.
The velvet suits look the same,
The speech still sounds like the music of Debussy,
    or Delius,
And grown men and women marvel at the range of thought,
The depth of emotion,
That the words convey;
But things are tougher now,
He decides that dreams are painful,
And takes pills to prevent them from disturbing his sleep.
Every morning he sets out with earmuffs, blinders,
And mittens made of stainless steel.
From his bathroom window he watches thousands of tiny
    rowboats lost in a storm,
And he wonders at their fragile forms, their suffering,
And he announces that he is a lighthouse
When they can see as well as anyone
That he looks just like them,
And it's all the same ocean, the same storm

POEM AT THE END OF THE SIXTIES

Sporting equipment disappears overnight
From the school gym;
Pretty soon the whole building goes

Poets and computer analysts are at a loss:
The Century Teaching Apparatus,
Consisting of books, assorted prophylactics,
And a few students as indicators,
Has been thrown out the window

DESERT RUN SCENARIO

You are caught pulling the brake,
Throwing pride and jealousy out at the back of the train;
People look as if they are startled,
They hadn't expected so much pain, and
The angel of death stops by, expecting to blow in
All the windows. You look up over your shoulder,
And ask it to please move on.
People look annoyed; they know by now
It's just another delay.

Your eyes move carefully around the engine,
Your shadow serves drinks in the dining car;
The light outside is dazzling,
And washes things red when you look at them

In the last town, you asked for some supplies
And were not understood.
The devil there was a dilettante,
With nothing much to offer
Except a passion for analysis
And self-deceit;
You aimed a crystal bullet,
You expected to shoot it clean through his clothing,
Clean through his heart,
But for miles all around cows turned to trumpets,
You saw the lost wagons of Death Valley, glazed blue
    with age,
Waiting patiently in another dimension
To be set free

You ran for days,
You managed to catch the last train out

SLEEP

You're trying to make some calls out
With the phone disconnected, there's not much you can do

You wear all your clothes, as if you are expecting guests
But you can't remember

The compass points four ways at once
But there is only one direction

In the morning, you are learning how to tap dance,
And it requires absolute concentration.
Others have been learning to make fire from stone,
But they may need a tap dancer too

Daylight moves deliberately, you notice that;
The room fills with objects you are hard pressed to recognize,
You imagine a city where the blind move like insects through
    the streets

THROUGH THE MIRROR

Inside are the props for a lifetime, whole rooms
In which to sit and watch plants grow
And a lot of circumstance that is lying around, inert
But inherently harmful

It looks simple enough,
You don't know much but people tell you everything is obvious;
You can kill off everything except for pride and paranoia,
And survive that way

On good days you see out just a little
There's a lake, and a shore where you find you've been
        standing all along,
A thousand mockingbirds, two long brown braids

It seems real enough,
But it's hard to define the substance surrounding you,
The incredible shapes, radiators
And the bodies of women

Everything you know is by accident;
You don't even recognize yourself, half the time

THE CONSUMING ANGEL

It's more a demon than anything else;
Fire couldn't kill it.
By way of introduction;
It will sever the nerve endings the way a thief cuts
    telephone wire,
Quietly, efficiently.
You are unaware of the visitation itself,
But it lasts a long time.
If you're lucky, it will leave sores on the inside of
    your mouth;
If you're lucky, when you wake up,
You know that something's wrong

You are holding on, you wake up
Holding on, your body relieves itself
The best way it can; you are sick for days.
There have been plenty of times when pain was the only thing
That set you apart from your shadow;
The light is different now,
You wake up looking for something that isn't lost,
An empty blue vessel;
It takes all your strength to fill it each time,
You know well enough it won't survive here

You wake up tired of running
At one hundred miles an hour
(Such speed is possible, if the pain is great)
There's a movie called "Nights In The Jungle,"
But you have lost all interest in metaphor

THE MOST SECRET ANGEL

for Andrea Behr

There doesn't seem to be an opening anywhere,
Not in anyone's world

People want to give it clothes to dress up in;
It gets a lot of business calls.

It's a fire covered with earth
And somehow it doesn't stop burning.
It's restless, and no one sees

I always look where it's pointing,
But I've never been able to feel its shape

I know it worries about surviving the winter,
But there's nothing I can do.
It wants to make a sound,
It wants to be contained

When it ventures out,
A feeling like the wind comes to claim its place;
Nothing fancy, just simple suspicion and fear

It has a hard time being honest
It can't say anything;
It wants, it wants

1.

Nothing settles, the fantasy life of pride
  meets February head-on,
Survivors build a raft but have forgotten what it means
  to set sail.
It's a world without horizons, and before I go to sleep
I place it, without much effort,
On the head of a pin.
The telephone rings, you want to know
About tomorrow, what time,
And I tell you all I've noticed, your absence,
The perpetual downward motion of rain

2.

There's no drama here, just February,
Its lack of illusions.
She said she was walking with webbed feet,
  with the most beautiful part of her hidden inside a shell.
She said she was sad, and you didn't understand it.
The telephone rings, the wrong end of the telescope this tim

3.

The days are like the last ones, and it
  gets so I can walk right through them
I never knew if it was the dark shape of a cloud or
  just an animal eating everything in sight in
  order to stay alive, I never thought to ask: were
  we really flying, was it really you?
Eight hours pass I forget to mention before I
  sleep again.

SPACE WALK / SELF-PORTRAIT

"the lightning and I had to pass together"
—Henri Michaux

I.

The world is flat
Nothing but horizontals, equations,
People talking in poems all around me,
Buildings that look like people

I want to die, so I can't sleep
I want to think, so I take a symbolic piss
This is not a space walk so much as a bathroom melodrama

2.

Late night in the big city and my neighbor the night-club singer
    is messing around with time
We come home at exactly the same hour, she looks like a cat
    who's eaten a canary, or maybe a pair of false eyelashes
She says she's never seen me before

I don't know what I must look like, the plane could have
    crashed an hour ago, there wasn't even a tree around to
    repeat the word "forever"
I'm wearing mostly white, but I don't think she wants to make
    anything of that

3.

Just about 4 A.M., and the town rides through the town like
    the dream of death that carried me home from the
    masquerade ball

We step through a door and the room becomes an empty
    canvas
We throw some kleenex at the mirror, slowly, one by
    one, as if they were real flowers, as if this were a real
    train we were on, the kind that always go

4.

Sleep hides me away
For another night.
A thousand razor blades sent up right away, and
    no idea how it happened

Peasants go by with thousands of years strapped to their backs
They're the first to tell me no one has a right to live,
They know I can't stay here, with the things I've stolen,
I can't return any of it

Their houses burn out from inside, and the birds all fly
    away

LOADED GUN

for James Tate

lots of murders and cartoon speeches

writing just once, and not making a copy

going where you can't be seen

silence, no color, no name

a book called translations

the scar on your hand, an ugliness of spirit

choosing things, like Ulysses or anyone, when all the time
the ocean is the answer

at the end of a good poem, a good sleep